HENRY KISSINGER, MON AMOUR

T0294315

Winner of the 2017 Frost Place Chapbook Competition

HENRY KISSINGER,
Mon Amour

poems

CONOR BRACKEN

DURHAM, NORTH CAROLINA

HENRY KISSINGER, MON AMOUR

Winner of the 2017 Frost Place Chapbook Competition
Selected by Diane Seuss

Published in the United States of America

Library of Congress Cataloging-in-Publication Data

Bracken, Conor
Henry Kissinger, Mon Amour: poems / by Conor Bracken
p.   cm.
ISBN-13: 978-1-4951-5768-4

Book design by F. H. Spock and Associates

Cover image:
Jenny Blazing
Overflow, 2017
acrylic & collage
30" x 48"
courtesy the artist
www.JennyBlazing.com

Published by
BULL CITY PRESS
1217 Odyssey Drive
Durham, NC 27713

www.BullCityPress.com

ACKNOWLEDGMENTS

Grateful appreciation is offered to the editors of the following journals, in which some of these poems have appeared, sometimes in different form and under different titles:

Adroit Journal: "Henry Has Me Tell Him About My First Time" and "Henry Makes a Suggestion"

The Chattahoochee Review: "My First Day in Argentina"

The Great American Lit Mag: "Oradour-sur-Glane"

Grist: "The Albigensian Crusade"

Nashville Review: "The Vulgar Luxury It Is to Be"

Puerto del Sol: "Henry Talks About the Hyenas"

Thanks to the many friends and mentors who helped me along the way towards this book, particularly Katie Condon, Kalen Rowe, Peter LaBerge, Kevin Prufer, Tony Hoagland, Joseph Campana, Sam Mansfield, Karyna McGlynn, Elizabeth Lyons, BJ Love, Woods Nash, Bryan Owens, and Austin Tremblay for their helpful and encouraging insights.

Thank you to Diane Seuss for her searing reading and sharp eye; to Ross White for his patience, perspicuity, and guidance; and to the Bull City crew for believing in this book.

I am sincerely indebted to Hamby-Lentz Solutions for the time and resources provided in Buenos Aires where preliminary research was conducted; to the Inprint Foundation and the

University of Houston for funding provided during the time some of these poems were composed; and to the University of Houston-Clear Lake for support during the time of the book's assembly.

Enormous gratitude to the Frost Place Board of Trustees for their enduring commitment to poetry as a living, vibrant art that requires nourishment and community they so generously provide.

Unrepayable thank yous to my parents for—among so many other things—goading me onto Wildlife Society and CLO trips, and, along with my sisters, for such unflagging support.

And, finally, Rachel—the only person who knows me well enough to know when I'm making it up: thank you for challenging me every day to dig the well a little deeper.

CONTENTS

"'Boohoo, boohoo,' Kissinger said,
pretending to cry and rub his eyes.
'[former Secretary of Defense Robert McNamara's]
still beating his breast, right? Still feeling guilty.'
He spoke in a mocking, singsong voice
and patted his heart for emphasis."

—STEPHEN TALBOT

THE TAO OF HENRY

Spend years in one spot on the hill
so the wind cannot reclaim it,

the wind that grabs at the space in your chest
your heart gives up

then takes back,
gives up then takes back.

Keep your boot on the throat of the season.
With your good eye dare the horizon to shrug.

A SHORT HISTORY OF OPERATION CONDOR

Previously, on "Days of my Sphere
of Imperial Influence," I was necking
with Henry Kissinger. We were standing
on the roof of a teetering glass building

in which two thousand companies daily outdid
each other in bilking the system that protected them
from the masses we could see from our perch
setting little fires on the serrated green horizon.

We fed each other delicacies with dirty hands—
dulce de leche under our nails, beefy
sinews between our teeth. We flossed
with the flags of every country but our own.

We bought islands we couldn't even stripmine.
We were white and alive and in love
with the little pulse in each other's wrist
that went give and take and give and take

and take take take take take take take. Take
my hand, said Henry. He was standing
on the grey parapet of my soul. I couldn't tell
if the heat I felt was the chlorine he'd poured

into my ditchwater eyes or the masses
combining their cookfires. I gave him my hand
and from each of the fingers he lopped off
with a damascene machete sprang

a smaller, whiter, shrieking hand.
They latched onto his and there we were:
together, doing what I called falling.
What he called curbstomping air.

ORADOUR-SUR-GLANE

The town rises like a welt on the windshield,
the windshield whipped by sun.

Hello summer, nice to be inside your fist.
Hello, Oradour, nice to meet you

and the memory of 642 people, gunned down
or burned to death inside a church.

Why come here, I wonder, as Henry
slams the coupe's door, says "we're here

for some perspective. To pay respects,"
as he strides off, shrinking so he fits

inside the *Centre d'Acceuil*'s door.
You go where death still lives

to remember you do too: live
where others haven't, breathe

where they were choked on smoke,
watching black ropes snare the stars.

Compassion is being aghast
at how beautiful the windows are,

still scarred with a crown of soot.
Empathy this horror at a ditch

in which someone was machine-gunned
which now is woozy with daisies.

MY FIRST DAY IN ARGENTINA

Here is Henry outside of Ezeiza:
rangy, wry, smile like a clay pot
lovingly repaired and Spanish fly
in the pocket of his summer-weight suit.

The sky blue butcher paper
on which thin cirrus bleed out.
I am happy to see him.
I am happy to be in a new country

where we will make our own country
with very precise exclusions.
We get into a taxi, zoom through
Capital Federal to a sandwich shop

among colossal hospitals. Later, the aphrodisiac,
but first two cocktails, one sandwich.
"*Sin tomate*," I'd said to the waiter
who by the veined marble bar

picks his teeth with a card
but there they are: tomatoes.
At Ezeiza in the seventies
a Peronist massacre. At the sandwich shop

right now, three tomatoes,
like the tongues of a dead Cerberus.
This is how assimilation works, I think—
by analogy. A scalar system of cognation.

"So the ex-president just died?" I ask
and he says, "yes, I miss my mother very much."
"How's it all been going?" and he replies,
"Look at this tomato ziggurat I've built.

Sometimes the clouds build a pyramid
in which they bury the sun."
"This sandwich is delicious."
"Yes. It hasn't rained here in a while.

My heart is heavy with the dryness."

HENRY PATS HIS HEART FOR EMPHASIS

which implies he has a heart.

I wonder what it looks like.

If it swivels behind and blanches white the saw-tooth wire fence
of his bones.

If it mutters to itself at night upset
by coups planned late, worrying that it left
the serial numbers on the submachine guns.

I hold his x-rays to the moon's blue light.

A piece of black fruit hangs left-of-center in his chest.

I've heard something walk around inside him
with measured steps that sound like
the distant thumps of cities being
brightly pacified

and this can't be it
though Henry swears it must be,

that shadow like a misshapen pineapple grenade—
"Each beat is an explosion shredding
the darkness death improvises its little bombs in!"

All I see is a low-light photo of a birdcage
with a shriveled apple wired to the perch,

because I think of his body
as a kind of orchard, each thump a pear
too tumid for the wind or branch to hold.
Because to me each beat's so sweet

it's overripe, falling suppurating to the earth
which absolves it of its rotting
by consuming it.

But Henry thinks of his body as a region
rebelling against oblivion's empire. A province
continually breaking away, a set of cities
in which his organs haggle over who
gets to spend tonight in the clock tower,

dragging unresisting alleyways and bridges
through the darkened hidden doorway of their rifle scope.

HOW AMERICAN

Henry and I, we're as American
as an overdose on opiates,

our bodies red and white and blue
and bloated. American as rural poverty

and tort law, fingers lopped off by gears
that move fast as the cruise missile in his living room

we take turns straddling like a mustang,
whispering hoarsely "ashes to ashes,

lust to lust." We preach from his porch
the gospel of metempsychosis,

of the transubstantiation of money
into status, and below us a horde gathers

the centavos we hurl like confetti
from a black metal parade. "Sunday date idea:"

he proposes, "we get The Pure Transactional
trampstamps together. Gothic script."

How I love him because he loves me
because I've accused no one but myself

for the nights drunk men have shaken me
down for sex. Because when my friends

get shot and surgeons lift their glistering
ruined viscera out of their bodies like fruit

too holy to be anything but burned
I want more not fewer guns, more not less

savage ammo to ram jagged knives of light
into the darknesses of the body.

I'm just trying to be honest with you.
I am striving towards a whiteness that's translucent,

and Henry, he says he can already see through me.
He says he knows that when I cower

under his upraised, liver-spotted hand
it's because I've already done something wrong.

That deep down I know why
I deserve this.

HENRY HAS ME TELL HIM ABOUT MY FIRST TIME

Something touches you
when you do not want to be touched
and it doesn't burn
but there it is—a wick.

The body a little bomb
that pleasure sometimes lights.

No Buick is safe
from the hand that reaches back
through that little gap
between the seat and B-pillar
to fumble softly at your ankle,

no complicated joint
with all its crisscrossing papery sinews
safe from the humid fire of a hand
sent through the dark
on the errands of need.

I lived in a swamp then, too,
jogging through August
along the crab-fetid ponds

and sometimes I beat him

but most times I collapsed
after vomiting what little water
my body allowed,
tangled up and ropy with bile,

and no matter which it was
he was always angry after,
smoldering,
the coarse dark hair on his arms and chest
miraculous for not just ashing away.

His body wicked, yes,
for how it bent me like an aspen to it

but also in the strangled breezes
that straggled off the sun-gilt estuary,
a swaying forest of fuses.

A stinking copse of ravenous wicks.

HENRY MAKES A SUGGESTION

I could. I could
make a canoe out of him.

His legs the oars, an arm the tiller,
the ribs and spine a sturdy frame over which

to stretch and batten the skin
I'll have to shave and tan and oil first.

The other arm a bony thwart.

What about the waters
long and deep and rough between us?

An outrigger, then. Scrap
the tiller and the thwart,

the arms booms now
fastened to the gunwales

and a leg of mine the float.

I can paddle towards you now.

I can eat the fish that nightly bob
up trying to chew me down to bone.

HENRY, CANOEING AMONG THE DANAKIL

After the class 3 rapids
the Awash river moves
like someone paid
close-to-nothing-an-hour
to stand monumentally still.

Henry ships his plastic oar
and floats
past a hundred head of cattle
lumbering beige and shapeless
among olive white-thorned scrub.

Two blue men in loincloths gape.
No one calls them savages.
Primitive.
Flotsam washed up
by the heaving tide of progress.

No one says jetsam
or that they've been passed over
by the selective hand of grace.
That there's no pocket in the sky
reserved for the halcyon lint

of their souls. That their voltage
is essentially human
but too impulsive
so let us convert it.
Who knows what they don't call him

when they step into his vessel
and jabber at each other.
If they don't call him anything.
If they can think of something
to think aside from

holy shit. Dude
what the fuck.
O tectonic blastula
and fetid tree bark
we are floating.

Who knows if
when they lift their hands at him
after he deposits them on the facing shore
like spare parts for a motor
his fuel is too refined for

they mean what he means
when he lifts his hand
to them: farewell.
Good luck.
May blight and death avoid you

for as long as blight and death can stand it.
And he watches them harass
their lump-backed cattle
into a semblance of direction.
And he cradles fondness like a newborn

drowning in the alien air.

HENRY TALKS ABOUT THE HYENAS

he once saw outside Harar,
and the men who fed them scrapmeat
from their mouths and of course

I think of language, of the tongue
and what we hang out of our mouths
because we want something to come

and wrest it from us,
to chew some meaning
out of the marbled half-discarded meat

but I'm always doing this—
making bad metaphors of moments,
trying to tape transparencies

over the shifting world
as it erases itself
a little bit at a time,

so here is the stone-walled city
brimming with yellow light
as night falls

crumb
by starry crumb
into the dusty cup of it.

Here's the dirty beat-up Nissan
Henry drives
out of the dented fortress,

the headlights that catch sixty eyes
like bright pennies
glowing underwater.

The raw red gobbets
held out to them
and the soft crunch

of stones as the hyenas approach.
Their mouths open like a book
in which terrible things are written.

"And the darkness?" I want to know:
"How would you describe it?"
"I'd say cavernous," he replies,

"but that would make every hyena's mouth
a cavelet, so let's go with velvety,"
and we like that.

The night a curtain
we can roughen with one hand
and smooth with the other.

THE MANY OTHER CARS OF HENRY

An eagle bald and throbbing

The condom god slips off and tosses just behind him on the steam-
    slick bathhouse floor

A diesel-powered rebel yell

Any thumb that settles princely down inside an eye socket's slick
    but vacant throne

The red horse of his voice that as it crosses all these promises off
    the register of silence foams whitely at the mouth,
    sand clogging up the froth

The piercing shriek a pig lets out when you ram it in the chute
    (which by the way he wants to pierce our tongues with
    a fetid bit of terror on our breath
    a whiff of death to keep our taste buds honest)

We drive over volcanoes sinkholes
tectonic cataclysms only he can see
because he does not think in minutes hours days

he sees in eras

the mountains shrinking under their burden of air
the glass cities hollowed out by winds and worn
down to inoffensive burnished nubs

he is a telescope it takes me
thousands of nanometric shifts
to aim precisely at the darkened stall of night

where I idle
gagging on the fumes
of waiting staying ready

because like Henry
to gain a millimeter on my opposition
I'd incinerate a yard

THE ALBIGENSIAN CRUSADE

Instead of the castles of the apostates
fallen open to the curiosity
of doves and wind and rain,

a bistro. The cassoulet umami-steaming
among little dishes of salt
and both of us a glass of wine, yellow

as a week-old bone.
Nothing "to *die* for," I assert
between gritted teeth,

eyes squinted under the huffing sun
as he takes my picture
in the light-flayed square beside the cathedral,

bangs writhing
in the breeze's sudden sieges.
Nothing a hill

I'd be willing to die on.
Nothing to kill for, no dish
holding a golden scepter

to lash a standard to
to drape over the world
and raze whatever doesn't match it.

Doing a *pas de deux* in the bishopric's winter
garden, the sun still zipping the river
up in a yellow body bag,

I tell him there was nothing
on that drop-leaf table
laid glittery with abstruse silver

to lose our heads over,
to keep a secret for.
Nothing for which to mobilize fur-pompous bureaucrats

on the holy office of our desire,
to have come back to us and say
as they did during the crusade,

"Here are their eyes,"
while opening a stiff leather pouch,
a whiff of campfire on his mink.

Saying, "At your behest
we gouged them all out

(save one, so they might see
the ineffable mercy of our army),

because if they believe this world a fiction,
then why would they need to see it?"

Nothing for which I'd ask him
to recant the canticle of his belief,

to sing backwards
out of a lipless hole,

unwind his concertina song
from the wind's bloodied, restless ear.

HOW MERCY WORKS

like the pearls that Henry gives me
when he feels bad for having needed
all the space my body takes
between him and the muzzle flash of orgasm

so badly he bruised my back or wrenched
my wrist or bloodied up this snout he rubbed
back and forth along the carpet's nap

the pearls which are just a glossy crust
of FUCKs an oyster layers over
whatever grit's got stuck inside it

a kind of beautiful pointing past weakness

or maybe it's like this creature Henry's trained to stagger
unsteady on its hind legs into my chambers

its pelt shampooed its balance wavering
something dangling bright and dangerous from its mouth

a platinum locket engraved with "I'm sorry
for what you made me do"

the creature whimpering like a cub
as I unthread the crimson ribbon
with which Henry delicately wired
shut its jaw

and weighting down the ribbon
a diamond ring
for this finger I broke by having

THE HANDS WITH WHICH HENRY PUTS THE CASUAL BACK IN CASUALTY

are delicate now and papery
like the precisely folded failure
of an origami master to approximate
with paper the mechanics of the human hand
which no one except the master
can see as exemplary of failure

this is not how Henry feels

if Henry feels it is the way a spy satellite feels
when it drops its roll of film towards the ocean
for a covert ship under cover of darkness
to pluck from the fluorescing whitecaps

a kind of mechanical vacancy   a whistling
not accounted for in the equations   it is
uncomfortable says Henry the way the breeze
works its fingers into the crevices and crannies
the engineers deny exist

                              uncomfortable
the way the wind assembles like a rifle a song
from the imperfections of the apparatus

HENRY AND I GO DANCING

and when he dips me in the sallow light
of the *milonga* no one gasps or gawps
or wonders who is which and does what
thing and this is how he likes it:

                              Anonymous,
innocuous, his hairdo just another choice
no one here has thought of making,
his grin a prologue to almost anything

but genocide. This is Buenos Aires, the year
[REDACTED] [REDACTED]-nine. I carry a revolver
in my waistcoat, a blade inside my cheek.
I am a psy-ops weapon not even sleep disarms

and Henry loves it. Henry ogles
as I saunter down the *avenidas*
salivating like a steak bleeding
on a porcelain plate. "O little station chief

of my heart. O my black site harlot how you
sparkle like a river over which the searchlights
of the helicopters sway and swoop.
Let our love be hollow-points in the war

against oblivion. My heart's your
Claymore mine so point it wherever
you need the blast to go." It's always
about explosions with him. He says

if I'd been alive when the bomb went off
I'd understand. And I say if I'd been
alive when the bomb went off
he wouldn't nibble at my ear like that

and he just laughs and laughs and laughs,
the sound of it like choppy water coughing
against a pier on which stands quaking
a shape I have not been trained to see.

THE RISKY BITS AND CURDLED BURSTS OF WHIMSY

is the name of the band
Henry wants me to assemble for his funeral.
Another February afternoon
by the runoff-heavy River Plate,

the sun smashing shadows out of everything,
pulverizing puddles into vapor,
the *desaparecidos* dropped from midnight sorties
turning in the turbulence the river makes

as it resists and fails into the sea.
Henry won't tell me what comes first:
the drum kit made from dampened cardboard,
the lead singer sinewy as jostled weasels and just as frothy,

the aftermarket pontoon boat I'll have to rent
to get us past the break to international waters,
but I know his death will come before
I incinerate him to cremains

I'm meant to scatter over slate gray waters
sloshing lawlessly with fish and distance.
I shudder when he says cremains.
The perverts lurking in the vegetation

yip a little when they see me shiver
and inside me fear and pity drop their brittle stalemate
to scramble over everything at hand,
brought up short when they both land

on the blinding flash a pair glasses
hiding dark inside the bushes makes
as it swivels towards me
scribbling in my notebook—

an ogle? a slack-loined rage? a look
burnished smooth of feeling by the sun
which Henry through bites of *choripán* swears
is not invited to his special day.

HENRY HAS A YEN

and asks if we can finance
terrorism tonight. He asks
if the white lady is dancing.

Little Chicken, lank-haired dealer
holed up in the hostel
a few blocks off the square

where couples tango for a couple
crumpled pesos dropped
into a velvet black fedora,

he wants to know if tonight
you've found the searchlights
pulverized and glittering

and bagged them into galaxies
the CCTV cameras probe for
with boxy glassy eyes.

We'll never ask you where
it comes from, or if you've cut it
with laxative or dish soap,

talcum powder, a dash of salt
or maybe flour. We like
the game of tasting how

you've tampered it to meet
the lengthy needs of rent
and food and next week's key.

And anyway, when we rub it
on our numbing gums
we don't want to think of

militias in the jungle, their dreams
of Simon Bolívar and cobbled streets
chest-deep in capitalist blood,

our heads bobbing towards the ocean
like the first boats of a swollen fleet
of trash-filled plastic bags.

The only cost we care to know
is cash—how many purple bills
you need from us embossed

with the heads of buried
bloated statesmen whose names
we pronounce like esoteric cuts of meat.

Pollito, call me
Condor. Little Chicken,
where's our fix.

CALL ME CONDOR

Of the many names that Henry calls me
call me this which suits me best—

my enormous wingspan, my rancid baldness,
my endless hunger for the dead.

Slightly threatened
and prone to living high.

Inside my vowels plays a video: me,
tethered to a bull that bellows

as I shred it into ribbons the watchers use
to lash their egos back to standing height.

I shred it unto death, the bull,
and then they free me from the carcass

for a couple years or so,
before dragging me from the air's blue throat

and tying me to a wooden frame
so they can take turns punching me from horseback

until I, too, die.
Pretty standard macho stuff.

But don't stop watching yet.
You need to see above me

my ragged brethren straggle in
and tighten to a stack of circles.

You need to see them
waddle up and crown me with their feasting.

How my favorite name devours itself.
How it's spelled with picked-clean bones.

THE VULGAR LUXURY IT IS TO BE

I summon up the vulgar
luxury it is to be
a chicken, dawdling along the fenced-in yard

and shitting willy-nilly everywhere.
It doesn't make it easier
to kill this chicken

but I do it—
wrench the head back, slit the jugular,
saw roughly through the windpipe.

I squat and watch
the blood drip into the bucket,
the body shuddering like a preacher

whose tongue got caught
in the electrical socket of God,
thrashing in the kind of ecstasy

that believes the darkness
is just another crease
in a cupped enormous hand

that carries all of us like water
rare and liquid through the dryness.
Today I am that hand.

And I say someone folded love
into the blade. That the appetite
which drags it back and forth

is a sacrament
even this chicken knelt to take.
I believe I am owed this.

That salvation can be willed.

ABOUT THE AUTHOR

Conor Bracken's poems, which have been nominated for the *Best of the Net* and received grants from Inprint and the Squaw Valley Community of Writers, appear or are forthcoming in *Adroit Journal, Forklift OH, Muzzle, The New Yorker*, and *THRUSH*. A graduate of Virginia Tech, a former poetry editor for *Gulf Coast*, and the assistant director of a university writing center, he received his MFA from the University of Houston, where he and his wife currently live.

ALSO FROM BULL CITY PRESS

LENA BERTONE, *Behind This Mirror*

TOMMYE BLOUNT, *What Are We Not For*

KATIE BOWLER, *State Street*

ELLEN C. BUSH, *Licorice*

ANDERS CARLSON-WEE, *Dynamite*

TIANA CLARK, *Equilibrium*

BEN HOFFMAN, *Together, Apart*

B.J. HOLLARS, *In Defense of Monsters*

CHLOE HONUM, *Then Winter*

ANNE KEEFE, *Lithopedia*

MICHAEL MARTONE, *Memoranda*

MICHAEL McFEE, *The Smallest Talk*

JILL OSIER, *Should Our Undoing Come Down Upon Us White*

MICHAEL PARKER, *Everything, Then and Since*

EMILIA PHILLIPS, *Beneath the Ice Fish Like Souls Look Alike*

ANNA ROSS, *Figuring*

LISA GLUSKIN STONESTEEET, *The Greenhouse*

ANNE VALENTE, *An Elegy for Mathematics*

LAURA VAN DEN BERG, *There Will Be No More Good Nights
Without Good Nights*

MATTHEW OLZMANN & ROSS WHITE, eds., *Another &
Another: An Anthology from the Grind Daily Writing Series*